Snakes in the Lobby

Scott MacLeod

MorningStar
PUBLICATIONS
16000 Lancaster Highway, Charlotte, NC 28277-2061

Snakes in the Lobby

ISBN #1-878327-76-3

Published and distributed by MorningStar Publications, 16000 Lancaster Hwy., Charlotte, NC 28277 USA. Phone 704-542-0278.

Snakes in the Lobby

TABLE OF CONTENTS

"For God does speak—
now one way, now another—
though man may not perceive it.
In a dream, in a vision of the night...
He may speak in their ears and
terrify them with warnings,
to turn man from wrongdoing and
keep him from pride,
to preserve his soul from the pit..."

Job 33:14-18

DEDICATION

Snakes in the Lobby is dedicated to
musicians and artists, and to all the people who
are called to work alongside these creative ones.

May our destinies be fulfilled in Jesus Christ.

May we ever bring glory and honor to the King
in all we do, and may we hear these words:

"Well done, good and faithful servant."

Special thanks to
Lyla MacLeod, my mother,
for all of your editorial help and
for all of the love and support
you have given throughout my life.
I love you!

FOREWORD

This little book has already sent shock waves through the Christian music industry. It should send them through the church as well. The deceptions and strongholds that grip much of the Christian music industry are only a reflection of what has gripped much of the church. We therefore felt that this should be published for the wider church audience.

Illustrations, such as the ones found in this vision, can be of great help as we try to discern strongholds of darkness. Just seeing and understanding a stronghold is half the battle in overcoming it. Satan dwells in darkness, so once the light has exposed his hiding place he is greatly weakened. I therefore believe that the illumination of many of the strongholds revealed in this vision is going to result in freedom for many.

In all things, we must keep in mind that we are not warring against flesh and blood, but against the powers of darkness. Those who are trapped by the enemy, even those who are being used by him, are not our enemies. They are victims. This vision is not intended to criticize or condemn anyone, but rather it is meant to help set people free. If the vision challenges you to examine something you are doing, do not get offended. Get free! Repent. To follow the ways of this present evil age will cost you more than the world could ever give you. As James stated:

> What is the source of quarrels and conflicts among you? Is not the source your pleasures that wage war in your members?

> You lust and do not have; so you commit murder. And you are envious and cannot obtain; so you fight and quarrel. You do not have because you do not ask.

> You ask and do not receive, because you ask with wrong motives, so that you may spend it on your pleasures.

> You adulteresses, do you not know that friendship with the world is hostility toward God? Therefore whoever wishes to be a friend of the world makes himself an enemy of God.

> Or do you think that the scripture speaks to no purpose: "He jealously desires the Spirit which He has made to dwell in us"?

> But He gives a greater grace. Therefore it says, "God is opposed to the proud, but gives grace to the humble."

Foreword

Submit therefore to God. Resist the devil and he will flee from you.

Draw near to God and He will draw near to you. Cleanse your hands, you sinners; and purify your hearts, you double-minded (Jam. 4:1-8 NAS).

Freedom begins with repentance. God does not forgive excuses; He forgives sin when we have repented. We will not be able to accomplish the Lord's purposes by using the many evil ways of the world that have crept into the fabric of modern Christianity.

We will never be able to reach the world by being friends with it. The fundamental nature of true Christianity is an affront and stumbling block to the basic nature of this present evil age. These differences we cannot change or compromise. As quoted above from James, to compromise with the world is spiritual adultery that can even turn us into enemies of God.

Even if we have been caught in this trap of compromise with the world, there is grace for those who humble themselves. We may think that we are in too deep and that there is no way out, but with repentance and humility, we will be led out of any trap that we have fallen into. We will be free! We will be victorious! What the enemy intended for evil will be turned into a greater good.

I have known Scott MacLeod for a few years now, and recognize him as a true knight in the Spirit. I believe that the message of this book is true, and it is vitally important for our times. It is not a sweet little bedtime story. Rather, it is a trumpet call to wake up, shake off the chains that are binding us, and take our stand for truth and righteousness.

Rick Joyner

PREFACE

The following is a vision that I received and the interpretation that unfolded regarding it. As this vision has left a deep spiritual imprint on me and has been truly life-changing, I pray and believe it will also be helpful to you, as well as to the many that have been confused, disillusioned and wounded by the condition of what is now called the Christian music industry. The vision was received while a small group of us were praying against the powers and principalities that have, and still do, control and manipulate this industry.

I believe this booklet will help us to understand and expose the real enemy. We spend much of our time and energy fighting, competing with, and criticizing the wrong enemy—each other. This is exactly what Satan wants. If we continue with this horizontal way of thinking and do not have eyes to see into the spiritual reality, we will not be victorious and will certainly not enter the fulness of our destiny as creative people in Christ. "For our struggle is not against flesh and blood, but against the rulers, against the authorities, against the powers of this dark world and against the spiritual forces of evil in the heavenly realms" (Eph. 6:12).

One further note: I believe many of the principalities that are exposed in the following pages are the same enemies that have plagued much of the church as a whole. The church has already been judged openly for some of this, but these dark powers are a constant threat. They still pollute and control many ministries, churches and individuals. It is critical that we identify these schemes of the enemy.

This vision also speaks of things to come. There is a beautiful new horizon dawning for those who will walk in the Lord's ways. The best is certainly yet to be, but there will be a great shaking and purifying before we see the light of this new day.

I have felt compelled by the Lord to put this down in written form. I encourage you to seek the truth that may be found in the following vision. As the Word says, "Do not put out the Spirit's fire; do not treat prophesies with contempt. Test everything. Hold on to the good. Avoid every kind of evil" (I Thess. 5:19-22).

Scott MacLeod

Part I:
The Vision

The Lobby

This is the vision: I was standing in a well-known hotel lobby, which I had literally stood in earlier that same day during a very well-known Christian music conference. In the vision the very large and open lobby was packed full, as it usually is, with men and women from all over. Many were artists, musicians or people directly involved in the business of music. The people were busy talking and going on with their business (what is commonly called "schmoozing"), each one dressed up in appropriate music attire.

Much to my astonishment and horror, I saw what looked like a massive snake lying on the lobby floor. I could not even begin to calculate its length, but it easily covered the full length of the room. Its fat middle was at least six feet in height and looked almost twenty feet in width. It looked totally stuffed. Amazingly, people were actually leaning up against it!

I could hardly believe what I was seeing. My first impulse was to yell and warn everyone, but I

Snakes in the Lobby

hesitated because no one else seemed to notice it—they just carried on with their business. Many people were surrounded, and some were even totally wrapped up in its monstrous coils, and yet they were still unaware. They all were in great danger. I couldn't tell if the people could not see what I was seeing, or if they had simply grown accustomed to this monster. It almost seemed welcome here.

I wondered, "Who let this thing in here? Surely the thing has to be dead for people to be standing this close to it and still be this comfortable with it."

Then it happened...IT MOVED. I couldn't believe that something that looked so heavy could actually move. But it did. It slowly poured itself in between a few groups of preoccupied people so as not to disturb anyone. It was silent, and no one saw it move. No one seemed to have a sense of danger. This was extremely confusing to me. It looked like many in this place, for some reason, had totally dropped their guard. Obviously, this seemed crazy because of what I was seeing. As I stood there, greatly perplexed by this strange scenario, I was suddenly struck with the terrifying sense that there were other snakes in the room.

I reluctantly and cautiously gazed across the room. We were surrounded! The oversized serpents were everywhere! As I continued to observe the

The Vision

situation, my emotions began to evolve rapidly from initial shock and terror into great frustration because no one else seemed to be aware of these snakes. Soon I was filled with a sense of compassion for the blinded victims, and finally an intense anger gripped me because these creatures had somehow infiltrated this place.

That was it. That was all I saw at first. But I knew immediately that the great snakes I had seen in this vision were the principalities and dark powers (or evil spirits) that have been controlling and manipulating much of Christian music. I knew I had seen exactly what the small group of us had just been praying about, and I told them what I had seen. It was as if a small movie screen had appeared before me and shown me these things, even in color.

This vision stayed with me for about 24 hours. I was surprised that it did. I guess I had hoped that what I had seen at first was the end of it, for it was not pleasant to dwell on. But it remained very graphic and the images would not go away. After starting to get literally sick to my stomach over what I had seen, my curiosity began to grow, and I began wondering what the meaning of it was. Believing there had to be a reason for this lingering scene, I finally began to ask the Lord to show me the full meaning of the vision.

He did, and this is what was revealed next:

The BIG One

I was taken back to the same lobby and was shown each snake in vivid detail.

The first snake that was revealed to me was the first one that I had seen earlier. It was definitely the biggest one, easily filling the full length of the large lobby with its great coils wrapped around everywhere. This greyish colored snake was so large that it took me quite some time to find its huge head. I finally spotted the head hiding in the twisted masses of the mammoth coils. It had a hollow and yet all-consuming look upon its face. One word came into my mind as I studied its massive head—HUNGER. I then observed that it had just finished devouring something, or someone. I instinctively knew that it was the latter. This snake was actually feeding on the people in the lobby, and still no one seemed to notice!

This serpent had the ability to slowly surround its victims with its enormous coils and then swallow them whole without them even being aware of it. I knew by its immense size and its lumpy and very bloated body that it had swallowed many victims. And much to my surprise, I could see the victims were still alive inside of it. They were moving around inside the creature's incredibly over-stretched belly. I could hear them still carrying on ambitious conversations with others in the lobby.

The serpent's name was "**Self-Promotion**."

Most of the victims did not know they had been consumed by Self-Promotion. But some, much to my dismay, had willingly and consciously allowed the snake to engulf them. The goal or intentions of these victims was the same as that of this bloated serpent—they all wanted to become bigger and BIGGER.

The Charmer

The second snake that I saw was to my left—a very beautiful-looking creature that almost made me forget the horror of the first. It was a type of chameleon, ever changing colors and appearance according to the desires of those under its power. It could look like whatever you wanted it to: male, female, young, old, innocent or seductive. It was swaying back and forth, doing a hypnotic dance. I found myself drawn to it, as were many others.

Suddenly I shuddered with disgust, for I knew this hideous thing. This was "**Lust**." I hadn't rec-ognized it at first, for it was incredibly charming.

There was a large group of people gathered all around it, and they were actually flirting and dancing with it, and with each other. Without even losing the rhythm of its cobra-like movement, Lust would strike its partners with a flash of fangs. With forked tongues that were identical to this serpent's ever-flickering tongue, the people spoke deceptive flattery to one another. They were starting to realize that they could use the power from this snake to gain attention and power for themselves. They could get what they wanted quicker by using the power of Lust. I realized that many of the victims that were now held captive in the belly of Self-Promotion had first been bitten and poisoned by Lust.

When one is first bitten by Lust, the venom brings a real high. But not long afterward, its victim becomes sick. Then often for relief, the victim keeps going back for another bite (for the venom is very addictive) until he or she is completely consumed with the poison. The victim in turn bites others, and the sickness spreads. I did not look at Lust for long, for I knew its enticing power was great and deadly.

Two Snakes

The next snake I saw was, in fact, two very long snakes. They were intertwined—wrapped all around each other just like snakes do when they are mating. This, by the way, is exactly what these were doing. One was red; the other was yellow. They were spinning over and over, making a very uneasy sound that pervaded the whole place. As they twisted and spun around, they appeared to be actually biting each other. All at once I understood that this writhing mass was "**Pride**" and "**Insecurity**." They were feeding off each other, and they were reproducing after their own kind.

Then I looked around the room and saw people who were turning yellow and then red. Yellow was the color of Insecurity and red was the color of Pride. People would change these shades back and forth just like the rotating colors of the spinning serpents.

The whole lobby seemed aglow with these colors. The two worked well together, though they also seemed to irritate one another. There was a nervous uneasiness building that made me want to scream. These two serpents made those who were affected by them (which was almost everyone, to some extent) feel miserable. However, they didn't want to admit it, because their pride told them that they might look weak, insecure or possibly unsuccessful. So the spinning continued. Pride, Insecurity, Pride, Insecurity, Pride, etc.

Flesh for Scales

I was surprised that I even detected what was revealed next. I knew it was only because the Lord was allowing me to see it—I never would have noticed it on my own. I spotted what had first appeared to be someone who had fallen down, but I saw that it was much too long to be human. It was hidden halfway under the front counter and was entangled among the feet of the people.

The reason I had originally believed it was human was because it appeared to have human skin or flesh. It had what looked like a human head. Though having the color of flesh and having no scales, it was obviously still a snake. It was very low to the ground and earthly.

This one was the "**Fear of Man**." It didn't have to do very much, because Pride and Insecurity were doing most of its work. It just lay there, moving its human-like head back and forth horizontally. Then I noticed that people all across the room were doing the very same thing, almost as if they had been entranced. They were only concerned about who was who, and how they were being perceived by others, so much so that they did not recognize the evil in their midst. This freaky creature blinded its victims from the holy fear of God and injected them with a deadly fear of man instead.

The Vision

People all across the room were so busy looking at each other that they were unaware that they had become entangled by the Fear of Man. It would subtly wrap itself around its victims' feet until they could no longer move; they were completely paralyzed with fear. I remembered the scripture: "The fear of man will prove to be a snare" (Prov. 29:25).

Up High

I then heard a movement above me. I instinctively looked up, and there, much to my distress, I saw another serpent wrapped around the balcony, its endless tail running down the length of the escalator. This one was bright green. It looked like one of those tree snakes—very comfortable with heights. This was "**Jealousy**," and it was literally green with envy. It was breathing very heavily and seemed to have fire in its eyes. I could tell it was burning up inside. I didn't want it to catch me looking at it, because I was afraid it was ready to explode with fury at any moment.

Jealousy attacked the high places. It couldn't stand to be down low. Its mist-like breath released a fog of competition which filled the room. I could see that those who had breathed in the mist, although they were chatting politely with their peers, now had that same fire burning deep in their eyes as did the green serpent. And I knew they would attack and tear down those in the high places in order to obtain these places for themselves. Many of these people had become easy prey for Self-Promotion as well.

On the Sidelines

In the middle of this confusion, my attention was drawn to a whole group of people standing off to the sides of the action—out of the reach of the great serpents. I was relieved, because I could tell they, too, recognized that there was something wrong here. They were talking among themselves and pointing toward the center of the room. I could tell that they were very upset about what was going on and about the way people were conducting themselves.

My eye suddenly noticed a swirling movement. The floor surrounding those who stood to the sides was alive. All around their feet were hundreds of small slithering snakes. I knew instantly that these were the offspring of Pride and Insecurity. These little serpents looked quite harmless in comparison to the big ones, but people were being bitten constantly, and with each bite they were injected with small doses of poison.

The Vision

The poisons were **"Bitterness,"** **"Criticism,"** **"Unforgiveness,"** **"Self-Pity"** and **"Self-Righteousness."** The more the people were bitten, the closer they would casually and fearlessly waltz up to the great Serpents. Some of these were the ones whom I had originally seen leaning up against the coils of these massive creatures. When enough of these poisons were accumulated together in a victim, it caused spiritual blindness—which was disastrous because these evil monsters could only be seen in the spiritual dimension. Thus the blinded victims became quite helpless and vulnerable to the enemy's attack. I was beginning to understand how so many people could unknowingly fall into the powers of the great Serpents.

The Helper

I started to cry out, "How can this be going on? This is a horrendous mess! How come no one sees this?"

Then to my surprise, a voice answered, *There is another snake that you have not yet seen. Look to your right*, he said. I was now approaching overload and really did not want to see anything more, but I did look, more out of curiosity than out of obedience or courage. I was expecting to be quite terrified, but I saw nothing except clusters of people deep in introductions and conversation.

Then I heard the voice say, *Look again... closer.* I wondered who was speaking to me. I heard the voice again, *Look closer and you will see.*

"Who are you?" I asked. I could not tell if the voice was coming from within me or from somewhere else. It felt like part of me, but I knew I was not just talking to myself.

I am the Counselor. And I am your Helper. I will guide you into all Truth, and even things that are yet to come, came the beautifully calming voice. Just to hear this voice, not to mention the wonderful words, set me at ease. I wondered how I could have such peace in the midst of such great turmoil. But I did. *There is no time to waste now. The time is short. I am with you always. You must see what I am about to show you. Look again... closer.* The voice spoke with a unique combination of both gentleness and authority.

So I looked. And this time I began to see it.

The White Snake

It looked almost invisible or transparent at first, but as my eyes focused it began to emerge—a totally white, brilliantly gleaming snake appeared. It was smaller than the others, but still of considerable size. It wasn't at all what I was expecting. It looked surprisingly pleasant and very placid. It had

The Vision

a kind of fuzzy light that radiated from it and filled the entire room. As I studied it further, it appeared to be good—almost perfect. It seemed so respectable and attractive that I had a hard time convincing myself that it was actually a snake that I was looking at. It had an inviting and yet strange smile on its face, with eyes sort of half-opened. This snake looked rather harmless and didn't seem to be attacking victims like the previous ones had. It wasn't bothering anyone.

Then I heard the same voice say, *Look again...closer.* So I did, and this time I began to see its smile transform. It looked as if it were mocking me. And behind that smug grin I began to see a horrid deception and evil. A chill ran up my back as I looked into its albino-red eyes. I could sense an overwhelming and unquenchable thirst for power and control. I began to see Pride, Insecurity, Lust, Jealousy, Self-Promotion and Fear of Man; virtually all the other snakes were hidden within this one, and by this one. As each evil that was contained within this seducer was exposed, it inflated in size, larger and larger. It quickly puffed up to six times its original size.

"**Religion**! This is the spirit of **Religion**!" I exclaimed, half with relief that its nature had been revealed. Yet I was disgusted that this one treacherous serpent could conceal so much evil.

Snakes in the Lobby

Intrigued, I thought to myself, "Could this be true? How could something that had looked this good and this virtuous be so desperately wicked?"

I suddenly remembered the other snakes that I had seen in the lobby. With an impulse, I swung around and searched intently for them. They were nowhere to be found. "Where are they?" I thought to myself. I tried hard not to panic, for I knew there is only one thing worse than the enemy, and that's the enemy that you can't see. Still not a trace in sight. I shuddered with frantic terror. "Where? I know they are right here somewhere," I told myself. I didn't dare budge.

A Fuzzy Light

I looked back toward the inflated white snake, and it too was gone. A fuzzy light now substituted in its place. I began to doubt everything I had just seen. "I must be losing my mind," I began to think. Everything looked normal in the lobby—orderly and prosperous. People were smiling, gracious and respectable. There was no sign of trouble.

Then unexpectedly I heard, "What will people think of you? They will think you are crazy for believing in make-believe monsters. Everything's fine. Everything is just fine here. There's nothing to worry about. There is nothing wrong here.

The Vision

Except you. You are the problem. You're what's wrong. This is a Christian function. Everything that is done here is done in the name of Jesus, and even for Jesus. You are the religious one. They'll think you're just insane, full of pride, rude, critical, jealous and too good for everyone else. Who do you think you are anyway? Do you really believe this nonsense? No one will believe you. Just look around you—you're outnumbered. You are losing your mind. Can't you see the success here? God is blessing this. Just relax. Be cool. You're too up tight. Go with the flow. Be a peacemaker."

I was ready to scream. Deep down I knew what I was now hearing wasn't right. It couldn't be—there was no peace in any of it. "Stop it. Stop it! That's enough. SHUT UP!" I had to silence this voice. I couldn't tell if it was coming from me, or from someone or something else. It felt like a confusing mixture.

In the distance I could hear a haunting chant, "Crucify Him, crucify Him!" What could cause such raw hatred? Then it all became clear to me. This was none other than the voice of "Religion," the same power that had gone against my Savior and had misled multitudes over the centuries into the most treacherous kinds of deception—Self-Righteousness and Religious Pride. This two-faced spirit causes people to do evil, or tolerate it, and all along believe that they are doing right and even doing God a service.

"I know I saw what I saw! And I know there is terrible danger and great evil here!" I reminded myself. "I have to see again. Why can't I see? The truth! I've got to see the truth. No more lies. No. NO!"

Your faith. Use your faith, came the familiar and much welcomed voice of my Helper.

"That's it—faith!" I exclaimed, amazed that I had almost totally forgotten about it. It was like a light being turned on in the darkness. I had been deceived and had let Fear of Man get a hold on me. I was no longer looking with eyes of faith, but with earthly vision, and it was futile. I was most sobered and horrified at the sinister deception Religion had cast upon me when in its presence—or under its spell.

"I've got to face my own fear. Forgive me for my unbelief," I beseeched the Lord. At that very moment, a great weight dropped off me.

You must be certain of what you do not see, continued the reassuring voice. Then I looked again. This time I mustered up as much faith as I could and I began to look with a renewed intensity. Sure enough, as I did, the whole brood of Serpents

The Vision

came back into view again—faintly at first, but with increasing clarity as my faith strengthened.

I felt a great relief, but it was the relief of a blind man who has recovered his sight while standing on a battlefield in the midst of war. I could now see a smooth, flesh-colored snake slithering away from around my feet. I shuddered with disgust, because I knew I had been slimed by this evil thing.

You must see with eyes of faith and not by natural sight, came the voice, *otherwise you are virtually blind.* I felt very weak and nauseated. Fear of Man had tried to suck the life right out of me. It had almost succeeded.

Now I understood how so many people could be blind to the precariousness of the situation that we were in. "Lord, forgive me for judging others who do not see." I surprised myself with this statement at first, but it seemed to just burst forth from my spirit. I was convicted of the fact that I had started to look down on others in the lobby who could not see what I was seeing. I had let pride slip in. "Please forgive me of my pride, dear Lord." My sin came into full view. "I am not worthy of your grace. Have mercy, oh Lord, for I am a sinner as evil as these Serpents. Apart from you, I have nothing good in me. I have sided with the enemy!" I was terrified of my own wickedness.

Snakes in the Lobby

Right then an irritating noise, that had reached great volume in my ears, stopped. I was stunned by the silence, and by the fact that I had not even noticed this sound until it had stopped. I could hear again. I remembered that this was the irritating sound of the two spinning Serpents, Pride and Insecurity, that was prevailing over the room. I had no idea that I was being so affected by their deafening sound.

I then heard my Counselor's welcomed voice speaking again with crystal clearness. *Pride comes before a fall. I must let you fall so you can understand the poverty of your own spirit. This is my mercy upon you. I must reveal the evil in you just as I reveal evil elsewhere. Nothing will be hidden if you continue in the light. My light is the truth. The truth is not always easy to receive because men love darkness. But it will set you free if you continue in it. Do you wish to continue?* inquired the gentle voice.

"Yes!" I replied.

Have you considered the cost? asked the Helper.

I somehow knew that to continue walking in this truth would cost me much more than I had originally planned on spending. After a time of pondering, I soberly answered, "Yes."

Reinstated

Then I saw a tall wooden structure towering over me. It was rugged and well worn—it was the cross. From it, as if in slow motion, fell a single drop of blood...precious blood...the blood of the Lamb that was slain. It landed directly on me. As it hit me, somehow this one drop of the blood washed over my whole being. I was washed. I was clean. I was free. I felt a great surge of regenerating power run through me. These words were spoken over me. *The message of the cross is the power of God unto salvation. You are forgiven, my son.*

At these words, I melted into a river of peace. I lost track of the amount of time that passed. All I knew was that I was being restored. I now understood that it is only by the grace of God that any spiritual truth, revelation or understanding is given to any of us. I also knew that this revelation would not be just for me. I was greatly humbled by this as I realized that to whom much is given, much will be required.

Now you will start to have real love—God's love—for the blind. You must walk in humility if you wish to walk with the Lord. Humility is the gateway to grace. God's grace is your divine help, and only with His help can you love others, for He is love. Remain in Him and He will remain in you.

Snakes in the Lobby

His love will never fail. I felt strength return. I felt rejuvenated.

I was reminded of these words: "The Lord is my helper; I will not be afraid. What can man do to me? For everyone born of God overcomes the world. This is the victory that has overcome the world, even our faith." These words were life to me. My confidence was renewed, my faith was set back in place, and my mind settled with great resolve.

I looked down and was surprised to see a sword held tightly in my right hand. It had blood on it—which was strange, because I did not remember striking anyone.

I could see that white imposter, "Religion," clearly once again. But now, its strange smile was replaced by an expressionless stare, and the once-brilliant white color was changing to a dull off-white. It lay there motionless, as if the lack of movement were its last defense against being exposed. I could see it smoldering with a murderous, demonic rage; but it did not strike. Strangely, it almost seemed afraid of me now. This was astonishing, because I knew Religion was the most devilish of all snakes—a master deceiver. It contained within itself all the evils of the others combined.

The Vision

It's because of the light, came a trustworthy voice, *the true light. Religion is afraid of the light because it cannot hide,* the Voice explained. *This serpent projects its own false light which confuses, distorts and deceives. The true light renders all of these powers useless. This snake was not afraid of you before, because it could hide in the darkness and deception within you. But as you confessed the sin in your heart and repented of it, you began to walk in the light. The true light is God's holy presence where no sin can survive.*

These were revealing and calming words to me, but I still did not know exactly where this true light that he spoke of was coming from.

The Armor

"Where is this light that you speak of?" I asked.

It is the light that is coming from the armor, was the answer.

I looked down and saw that I was wearing a suit of armor and holding a powerful sword. Both were shining brilliantly with a glorious light, which made that fuzzy light (which I now knew was really no light at all) look pitiful and cheap. I was amazed. All along I had been aware that I was being protected, but I had not been conscious of wearing this armor, although I was incredibly relieved to find that I was. I knew it was only by God's grace and mercy upon me that I was allowed to wear such heavenly protection. But I was surprised to see that it fit me so perfectly. It was not cumbersome nor heavy. It looked and felt as if it had been made just for me.

It was made for you. And it is yours. For this is your destiny in Him, spoke the Counselor.

As I heard these words, I became aware of other bright lights that were moving throughout the lobby. I was surprised that I had not seen these earlier. I recognized that the true light was coming from all those who were girded in brilliant armor. They each carried swords in hand. I was overjoyed, because I knew that they too were aware of the evil in the room. Much to my amazement, the snakes were afraid of these armored ones and would actually avoid them, for they had been given great authority. I breathed in a deep sigh of relief. It was so good to know that I wasn't alone in this.

*This is the full armor of God that you and your fellow soldiers are wearing. It consists of the Helmet of **Salvation**, the Shield of **Faith**, the Belt of **Truth**, the footwear of the Gospel of **Peace**, the Breastplate of **Righteousness** and the Sword of the*

The Vision

Spirit—which is the **Word** of God. *When these are fitted into place, there is a glorious light that is projected. You must be dressed with the full armor in order to stand against the great deception and evil that you are now well aware of. And you must also pray in the Spirit on all occasions with all kinds of prayers and requests; otherwise, you are vulnerable to the enemies' attacks, and will certainly fall prey to their many powers.*

As I heard this, I began to study the people in the room more closely, and was stunned to find so many without armor or weapons. This was obviously a war zone, yet many people were not dressed for battle, not even self-defense.

Some people had the armor on, but it was very tarnished and dull. This confused me, because I knew the full armor was supposed to shine beautifully. These people looked worn out.

These are the ones who have not taken their swords out of their sheaths in a long time to defend themselves against the Serpents. They have grown weary and are defeated, came the wise voice. *They are not yet under the full control of the serpents, but they are not walking in victory as they were destined to do.*

I noticed that their armor was very loose, and they were in danger of losing it at any time because of constant attacks from the enemy. Yet they still did not take out their swords to fight back. What I saw next really spooked me—I saw one of the small poisonous snakes named **"Bitterness"** slip under a loose breast plate of one of the soldiers. There it stayed hidden under the armor. The warrior was not even aware of it! He had on the full armor, but his armor did not shine. I could tell by his sour countenance that he was holding unforgiveness and resentment. He was being eaten from the inside out.

There were also many people who were missing parts of their armor. Some had lost their swords, and some had lost their shields. Some were missing breast plates, helmets, belts that held the armor in place, and so on. There were all different configurations of equipping—or lack of it. Many people, I noticed, were missing Righteousness and Truth. But to be missing even one of these pieces could be disastrous, because the enemy was relentless in hitting the exposed areas. Wherever there was flesh, the snakes would inflict wounds.

Finally, I saw some people who actually had no armor at all. This was totally ridiculous. They were "sitting ducks"!

I looked down at my armor again. I didn't remember when I had consciously put it on. It still seemed strange to be wearing such noble equipment, knowing the great deception and sin which dwelt within me. I was afraid that it might have been given to me by mistake, or that I had acquired it dishonestly. I did not feel worthy of it at all.

The Blood and the Sword

You are not worthy apart from the blood—the blood of the Lamb of God who takes away the sin of the world. But because of it, you are made worthy. The blood has washed you clean. Everyone who has received the blood has this heavenly equipment waiting for him. It is the Lord's will that this armor has been given to you, not only so that you will be mighty and victorious, conquering evil and doing great exploits for His kingdom, but mostly so that the Lamb Himself can be seen in you. For when you wear the full armor, you become like Him.

By God's grace you also have chosen what is right and good—to put on the full armor. As you have seen, some who have the blood still choose not to wear the armor. Some wear only a few pieces, but it only becomes glorious when one is fully clothed in it. As you wear it, you are clothed in Christ: He is your Salvation and your Righteousness, He is the Truth, He is the Word, He is

Snakes in the Lobby

the Good News of Peace, and He is the very essence of your Faith. Each one has a choice to be fully clothed with Christ, the voice explained.

I then noticed again the crimson blood on the sword that I was still holding. I was curious about this. I assumed that this must be the enemy's blood—though I didn't know when I had ever really engaged the enemy or drawn any blood.

This blood has been applied to your sword as you have fought the good fight of faith. It is not the blood of any devil, beast or man. This is the only blood that will ever touch your sword. It is the blood of the Lamb, came the faithful voice. *This is all you will need for victory. Remember that your struggle is not with flesh and blood. Satan and his Serpents will not engage with you in battle when they see the blood and the sword, for they know they have already been defeated by the blood of the Lamb and by His Word. They cannot stand against this kind of power. They have already been judged and condemned by the Righteous Judge—and their doom is sealed for the appointed time. As you submit and fully surrender your life to God, you will have all the authority you need to resist evil, and it will flee from you.*

I will show you how to use the sword. You must remember that your sword is not to wound or kill, but to heal and to bring forth life. This is the sword of Truth. It is the Word of God. It will divide and sever between good and evil. As you learn to use this sword, my Word will become your word, and your word will become a sword. With your words you can wound or heal, build up or tear down, bring death or life, bondage or freedom. You must never use your sword to inflict injury or bondage on your brother, but only use it to set captives free.

If you use this sword you will never be blind, for you will walk in the Truth. Its brilliance will ever bring light to your path. But if you do not use it, you will most certainly be overcome by the great deception of this dark hour. With this sword and your shield of faith, and with my help, you will be able to cut your way through all darkness.

And above all, you must learn to love—just as Christ has loved you. To pursue truth and love will be the hardest battle you will face. Let love and truth conquer you. Then you will have conquered the enemies of your soul. This will be possible because I am in you. And I am Truth and I am Love. Go forth and **speak the truth in love!**

Purity

Just as the serpent led Eve astray by his cunning deception, there are many cunning Serpents today *who seek to deceive you and trap you in their wicked ways. Therefore, you must be sincere in your purity of devotion to Christ. He must have first place in your heart—**your first love**. Seek Him with all your heart. Anything short of this kind of commitment and loyalty to Him, and you will surely fall prey. Remain in Him, and you will become pure. You will partake of His divine nature. You will be clothed with Christ. Seek nothing less than the purity of Christ, God's perfect Son. For it is written, "**Be holy, because I am holy.**"*

"Pure and holy!" I exclaimed. "I am anything but that!" These words seemed totally foreign to me. I could feel myself getting discouraged, knowing that I could never live up to this standard. I realized that these were things that I rarely even thought about. It was an offense to my flesh!

One day you shall be like Him. Therefore, everyone who has this hope in Him purifies himself, just as He is pure. Everyone who cleanses himself will become a noble vessel, made holy and useful to the Master, prepared to do any good work. To the pure, all things are pure. Do not worry or be burdened now. You need only to cooperate with Him in this good work. Your Father will be faithful to complete what He has started in you. He will do it!

The Vision

"But how do I begin to seek this purity?" I asked.

Purify yourself by obeying the truth. His Word is truth. There was silence for a moment. And then the Helper continued as if He were whispering some secret wisdom. *If you are HUMBLE and TEACHABLE, God will do immeasurably more than you could ask or imagine.* Then He spoke in a most reassuring voice. *Do not be disheartened; I will help you. Don't try to figure it all out—just humble yourself before the Lord, continue to spend time in His presence, get to know Him, and you will fall deeply in love with Him. For to know Him is to love Him. Only then can you learn to obey. For once you love Him, you will obey Him. Love never fails!*

This is the high calling of God. You are to live a life worthy of the gospel of Jesus Christ—a life of love. Pure love. Do not be overwhelmed. It is a daily walk—one day at a time. Every day you must deny yourself, pick up your cross, and follow Jesus your Lord.

I started to relax, and again a wave of great peace washed over me. I began to rest in the fact that holiness and purity are my destiny in Him, and everything that He has declared over me will come to pass. I need only to trust and obey His good Word.

Love and Forgiveness

You will need a new type of love in order to go on any farther. Your love for the Father has been seen; and there is nothing that makes Him more pleased than seeing you learn to love. But you now need His divine love in order to continue on in this journey. It is a love that blesses even when cursed. Presently you love those who love you. This is a shallow love—and it is earthly. For your love for the Father to be perfected, you must learn to love your brother (there was a pause) *and your enemy. Do you desire this kind of love?*

"Yes I do. I would like to learn to love as the Father loves." I replied with as much enthusiasm as I could muster up, considering that my feelings had just been hurt as I realized that my love was perceived as shallow, at best, by all of heaven. But I somehow knew this was the truth, and I really wanted to change. "What must I do to learn to love like this?" I questioned my Counselor.

You must learn to forgive...and pray for those who have offended you or hurt you, was the answer. There was silence. I don't know for how long. But I knew in my heart that to really love like this would cost me much more than ever before, and it would take great faith in the Father. This was a new dimension, like a great door that was opening before me, with a vast and wonderful horizon ahead.

Forgiveness is not easy, but it is required. At times it will be painful. Are you willing to enter into this suffering? asked the Helper. I knew by this point that I would be a fool to go back, for I could see the beautiful and glorious horizon before me.

"Yes," I replied, rather surprised at my answer. But I felt a divine empowerment as I said it.

Good. When you learn true forgiveness, you will learn true love.

Right away I was taken on a journey through my memory of people whom I had not forgiven, or not fully forgiven. With a supernatural help, I was able to forgive many people. I also asked the Lord for His forgiveness for the wrongs that I had done to others, knowing I would have to go personally and ask the same of some of them. It was very intense. I had to face fears, anger and hurt; but when it was done I felt free. And much lighter.

You are forgiven as you have forgiven.

With tears I began to thank the Lord for His great love and forgiveness. These two words, Love and Forgiveness, had a whole new meaning to me now. They were precious. They were heavenly. They were real.

The Brotherhood

*There is one more thing that must be done. **It is not good for you to be alone**. No one will see victory in the days to come if he stands alone. You will need true brotherhood,* stated the Counselor as He brought one of the shining warriors over to me. *It was right for you to confess and repent to God when you were convicted of sin, but you must also learn to confess your sin to your brother. You must learn to pray for one another so that you may be fully healed, because your brother is part of you, and you a part of him. If you are honest and real, you will sharpen one another and you will have fellowship. This is part of what it means to walk in the light.*

I felt strong hands placed on my shoulders. The noble warrior, my brother, now standing next to me, was praying for me. It was humbling at first, but as I began to confess my sins to him, we were surrounded with an ever-increasing glorious light. The light became so bright that I could hardly see. Much to my astonishment, he totally identified with me and understood my struggles—and even the sin which wars against my soul. For he had some of the very same struggles as I.

We began to openly share our hearts with each other. I felt safe and understood. Then I prayed for him as he had for me—for his weaknesses to be perfected by the Father's power. We were refreshed, renewed and invigorated. We laughed together for some time and then began to spar with our Swords of Truth. He was very good. He had some moves I had not seen before, but I stretched him with a few moves of my own. We challenged each other, spurred each other on, and sharpened one another with our Swords of Truth. As I sat down to catch my breath, I realized for the first time just how badly I needed brotherhood. To be alone in this war would be crazy. We needed each other.

We then committed to love and serve our great God and King, and to love and serve each other. We were comrades. We were in this thing together—through thick and thin we would defend one another. I was starting to understand my purpose and my mission—*our* mission.

The Black Snake

Suddenly I found myself again surrounded by the bizarre activities in the now all-too-familiar lobby. However, this time I was excited to meet and talk with some of the other armored warriors, for I knew that there would be others that I would be strategically connected with. Just then, I was interrupted by something I saw out of the corner of my eye. It was lurking in the shadows. I thought I had seen it a few times before, but I had never been able to identify what it was. It seemed to vanish each time I looked in its direction.

But this time I saw it. It was pitch black. I saw the tail of a great black serpent. The snake moved swiftly out of sight as if it sensed that it had been seen. I was certain that I had spotted it once before outside the large glass windows in front of the hotel. I probably hadn't paid it much attention earlier because of the horrors I had been seeing inside at that time. Now it was on the inside of the building. I could not fully see it, but I knew it was here. It kept well hidden in the dark shadows and corridors.

Right then a terrible darkness and sense of hopelessness swallowed the atmosphere of the entire lobby. It was accompanied by a horrible stench, like something was rotten. This foul atmosphere came in so quickly that it took me off guard. Like a thick black cloud, it smothered the place. It was sickening to me, and I began to fight deep depression. I felt heavy—so heavy that I could hardly even hold my head up. My shoulders slumped over. I started to remember every disappointment in my life. I felt so sorry for myself I could hardly move. I stared at nothing for a good

The Vision

while and then sank down against a wall. There I sat—lifeless.

"What is the use of going on?" I thought to myself. "There's no use. No hope. Why live with such pain?" Everything started to look fake and meaningless—almost as if it were made of paper. Despondency set in. I looked for help, but I could see others throughout the room who were slipping into a state of utter hopelessness, too. "Where were my friends? The other warriors?" I felt totally alone. I was isolated. I began to despair of life itself. I wanted out. I was tired of fighting...so tired.

The grief was unbearable, and I found that I could hardly breathe. I felt like I was at a funeral. But whose? "NOT MINE!" I shouted as I shook myself awake. "Away from me! In Jesus' name, away!" I cried out with all my might. "JESUS!" At once the stagnant cloud of darkness began to lift off me.

I stood up, took hold of my sword and swung it three times as I declared, "I have been given life, and **life abundantly**!" These words and my sword sliced through the thick depression, and I felt the regenerating breath of Life return to me. My heart filled with a tremendous sense of gratitude. I became deeply thankful, and I praised my Lord. I began to thank God even for all the hardships and disappointments of my life. Looking back now, I could see how it had all worked together for my good. As I praised Him, I could see that He is ever faithful, and that He works out all things in accordance to His will. I began to rejoice and to pray and give thanks for all circumstances. I lifted my shield of faith. I knew that nothing could touch me now. The cloud had totally departed.

Coming back to my senses, I remembered the black snake that I had seen earlier. I knew that I was somehow being affected by this grim and well-hidden serpent. I still could not see it, but I had surely felt it. "What was this dark power that had come over me?" I wondered. "It's killing me. It's killing others!"

As I pondered what this could be, these words came to me: "**The wages of sin is death**" (Rom. 6:23). Then I knew that this unilluminated serpent was none other than "**Death**." It was circling, or more accurately, stalking the place—stalking me, or anyone it could find and swallow. I knew that death is the wage that is earned when sin is allowed to continue and fester. Sin full grown gives birth to Death.

"This must mean spiritual death and not literal physical death," I said to my trusted Adviser, trying to talk myself out of the reality of death looming.

The Vision

Which is worse? I was answered with this question. I was silent. Then before I had time to reply, the answer to my question came. *There already has been both physical and spiritual death. Sin affects both realms—the natural and the supernatural.* I knew this to be true, for I had seen death strike before, even among these people—and I would never forget it. But it was always easier not to think of death or punishment as being something so real, so final, as physical death. And yet, now I realized that spiritual death is the true finality, for it affects the eternal realm.

It is always easier to dismiss death as something else, than to face the fact that our sins will find us out. I was again reminded of the truth that **"a man reaps what he sows."** Be they good or evil seeds, it is just a matter of time and there will be a harvest, for God cannot be mocked. This is His law of creation. This harvest was ripe for reaping, and I feared that many of the seeds sown here had not been good seed.

I knew that something had to be done. And soon! This was getting insane. Things could not go on like this. There already was great bondage, and even "Death" now was crouching at the door.

That is why the snakes are being revealed, announced the Counselor. *Judgment is also at the door. The Lord will judge all sin. He has allowed the people to continue in their wicked ways—that is His judgment. He will soon shake everything that is not built upon the only true foundation—the Rock, which is Jesus the anointed one. The one who hears His words and puts them into practice is the one who builds upon the Rock.*

The Snake Keepers

As I gazed back out into the busy lobby, filled with a strange blend of both natural and supernatural interaction, I wondered again, "How did these snakes get here, and how did they get so unbelievably huge?" I knew that snakes, like all reptiles, grow in size throughout their entire lifetime, unlike mammals which reach a certain age and then stop growing. Therefore, judging by their size, one could conclude that these creatures had been growing here for quite some time. They undoubtedly started off small and seemingly harmless. But I still did not understand who let them in here.

That's because you haven't seen the Snake Keepers yet, came the voice.

"Snake keepers!" I exclaimed. "Where?"

Watch closely, was the reply.

The Vision

I watched, and this is what I saw next. I saw at least a dozen shadowy figures, that I assumed to be human, moving as fast as they could back and forth. They were breathing heavily and sweating profusely. I could tell that they were under a tremendous amount of pressure and stress as they labored, using shovels and wheel barrows to transport mounds of something that appeared to be dull green and gold in color.

Much to my dismay, they were actually *feeding* the snakes—sometimes using their shovels to feed the serpents directly and sometimes dropping the feed off in piles next to their hideous jaws. In either case, it was devoured instantly. The beasts had furious appetites for this stuff. I now realized how these Snakes could have grown to such an enormous size. This seemed totally insane to me. Why would anyone want to feed such terrible evil? It was like feeding fuel to a fire. "What is this feed, and who are these guys now?" I wondered with much frustration.

*The snake feed that you see is **money**.* That explained the greenish gold color I had seen. *The shovels and wheel barrows that they are using are the tools, or ways, Of the World. The darkened figures are the Snake Keepers. They have become the **Slaves of Greed**.*

Snakes in the Lobby

I then began to hear a clattering sound. It was the sound of chains. Much to my astonishment, each of the Snake Keepers were bound in heavy irons, but what I saw next is what really shocked me. The slaves where chained to the massive coils of the great Serpents themselves. I couldn't think of a more precarious or vulnerable predicament to be in. They were at the total mercy of the Serpents. And I doubted that mercy was something these Snakes would ever be known for.

As long as they were kept well fed, the monsters remained relatively still. But if they began to grow hungry, they would begin to shift their menacing coils, causing the chained slaves to be thrown and dragged around like rag dolls. I then noticed a few empty chains still connected to the snakes, but with no one attached to the end. I was relieved to see that it looked like some of the slaves must have escaped or been freed somehow. A few had probably escaped, but then I observed that the end of some of the chains which had once held a prisoner were now twisted, severed and broken links. It hit me that some of the captives had actually been eaten by the giant Serpents. These Keepers had not been able to keep up with the grueling pace of keeping the snakes fed.

I understood now that the Snake Keepers were the ones who originally welcomed or permitted the existence of the snakes in this place. They once thought that they could control the Serpents and use their powers for their own gain and for the "goodness" of their cause. The fuzzy light of "Religion" had distorted their vision, and they too were deceived. But the seemingly harmless reptiles grew so quickly and became so powerful that the Keepers were now under their control, and were working frantically to keep them fed. I was reminded of the scripture, **"For the love of money is the root of all kinds of evil"** (1 Tim. 6:10).

You can only serve and love one master. You will love one and hate the other. There is only one Master who is full of love and justice. The other, as you now see, will inevitably devour you, added the voice. *All men are slaves—either to righteousness or to sin. A man is a slave to whatever masters him.*

A Misleading Parade

What I was about to see next was actually heard first. It was the sound of a song, or songs. It sounded like many voices, and yet somehow like one voice. It sounded like many instruments, and yet somehow like one. It was very appealing—a sing-a-long type, joyous, upbeat and seemingly innocent melody. But then it would change tempo into a slow, seductive progression which moved into sad and even depressing sounds. Then it would whirl into a bombardment of aggressive and violent sounds. It was ever-evolving, causing a wide variety of emotions.

Then it came into view. It looked like a parade that came marching through the very center of the already crowded lobby. It looked strange and yet hauntingly familiar. My attention was immediately drawn to a tall, colorful figure who was leading this procession. He was at least a head and shoulders above everyone else. He was a very intriguing character, dressed somehow in every color and style one could imagine—both old and new. He had a precise and prominent walk; each of his steps and movements seemed very well calculated. He was fascinating to watch. He moved so gracefully it made me not want to take my eyes off him because I didn't want to miss what he would do next.

I then saw that he was actually playing an instrument. It looked like a flute but I knew it was much more than that. Out of this one individual, and from this one instrument, originated all the songs and sounds that were leading the procession, which I was now hearing at an increasing volume as it approached. There was so much activity and excitement it was overwhelming. I felt an intense urge, almost like the pull of a great magnet, to

The Vision

jump in line and follow along. Something told me not to.

This colorful figure had immense power to influence people. I had never seen anything quite like it before. There was a long line of colorful people who followed behind him. They were dancing, singing, acting and playing all kinds of instruments. They were all dressed up and wore all kinds of styles, colors and hairdos. Many resembled popular secular artists of today—some were almost look-a-likes. You could tell that the performers actually thought they were quite unique, but it was clear that they were really just imitating the leader. Each tried in his own way, but still there was a tremendous amount of conformity to whatever kind of pace, style and sound this leader was emitting.

Every once in a while this lively leader would actually stop playing his instrument and shout out something. Then he would immediately start into a new song. The entire parade would frantically try to change the way it expressed itself—some would even begin to change clothes and styles. Their songs and sounds would change as well. The tall guy would let out a great bellow of laughter as the entire parade would scramble to conform to his leading of what had now become a very haunting song. When they had just about conformed their music and expression to his, he would again change, sending the whole mob into mass confusion. Each one was trying desperately to hear the newest sound. It was a mess.

The people in the crowd were very rude to each other, pushing, shoving and even stepping on those who had fallen down—all trying to move themselves to the front of the procession, and then having to exert all their energy to try and stay there so they could be the first to hear the new songs and expressions. Except for a few at the front, many of these people seemed quite frustrated and tired. I began to notice that even the ones at the front, after a short time, would start to look miserable and empty. Yet they all kept up this grueling pace. They seemed totally entranced as they were driven to get a position at the front. The scary thing to me was that I didn't think many even knew that they were following this tall minstrel. Perhaps it was because of the familiar fuzzy light that hovered over this procession.

Then without warning, the tall figure grabbed two of the performers closest to him and lifted both of them into the air, one in each arm. And with enormous strength he started to juggle them. He threw them around like dolls, higher and higher into the air. The whole place was now in an uproar. I couldn't tell if people were cheering or screaming. I think both. The higher the artists flew into the

The Vision

air, the louder things became. It was great entertainment. It caught the attention of everyone, but I feared that someone was going to get hurt. Even the Snakes were watching.

Then what I feared happened. The leader, after hurling the figures high into the air, suddenly pulled back without catching one of them. There was a shriek. The artist fell to the ground with a thud, I am sure, but because of the uproar I could not hear it. The other one was half caught and then quickly thrown aside. A horrid laughter burst from the lips that were now preparing for the next haunting melody to be processed from the flute. The wounded artist was trampled under a myriad of ambitious feet.

As the tall figure started into his next song, he began to nod at each of the Great Serpents as he led this flamboyant procession around the packed lobby. This seemed to be a nod of greeting or acknowledgment. The Great Serpents would actually stop all activity and nod back in return as if to show respect to this tall minstrel—something I thought I would never see from such savage beasts.

"Who is this fellow that could demand respect even from these evil creatures?" I really didn't want to know. It was as if he and the Snakes were in on this whole thing together.

The Pied Piper

*This is the "**Pied Piper.**" You know who he is.* The Counselor seemed to always know what I was thinking.

Deep down I really did know who this was. I just didn't want to acknowledge it. It was too wicked to think of—too disturbing.

He has always been a master musician—since before his great fall, informed the Counselor.

"But how could he have such control over all this...and over all these people?"

The songs that you hear him playing are the songs of Babylon—the songs of the world. Many of these people in the parade are true sons of God who have been given the gift of creativity. The Piper has held creativity captive for many years now. This is because the sons of God have looked to, imitated, and chased after the creativity of the world. They have not looked to their Creator for His divine expressions to flow through them. As you can see, they are now under a curse. They have become the tail and not the head.

The ways of the world are opposed to the ways of God. These creative ones have fallen short of God's original purpose and intention for them and

58

The Vision

*their gifts. Instead of being a light to the world, they have become **like** the world. They have not worshiped the Lord their God with all their hearts. Many have stolen glory for themselves and have not given the glory to God—they have instead used their gifts for their own gain. They have worshiped and served worldly things: prestige, popularity, money and even music itself. They love and listen to the praises of men more than the praises of God, and with divided hearts they have strayed from their first love and have become easy prey for the Great Serpents and the leading of the Piper. **All true creativity and true worship must be an honest expression of the heart.***

This was too sad to watch anymore. I looked away. My heart was broken for them. I knew all too well what kind of power they were up against—for I now realized that I, too, used to march in this same parade. Only now from this viewpoint could I see the serious delusion these people were under and how far off track from God's original purpose the Piper was leading them. I could not blame anyone, for I had already spent my time in there striving for the front. Now I wanted so much to warn them.

The Piper knows very well the tremendous power of music and the arts, explained the Counselor. *True creativity, when given fully to glorify and*

Snakes in the Lobby

to worship God, is one of the most powerful weapons known in heaven and earth. That is why the Piper is fiercely determined to control it.

Then I heard a Voice pronouncing above all the commotion, ***Come out. Come out of her, my people, so that you will not share in her sins, so that you will not receive any of her plagues; for her sins are piled up to heaven, and God has remembered her crimes.***

I pondered these strange and powerful words. I knew they spoke again of Babylon—the ways of the world that had infiltrated these people and inspired their songs. One thing that I knew was that these words were timely and urgent. It was like a siren going off.

The last thing I saw was people, one by one and in small groups, starting to drop out of the parade. This parade that had once seemed to be so unified was now starting to divide and fragment. I believe some had heard the Voice and were responding. Others dropped out more because of frustration, or to look for other opportunities. The rest marched on. I looked at the Piper one last time as he passed by me and turned. I noticed something slipping out from under his colorful attire. It was the tail of a Snake!

Clean the Inside First

After seeing all these things, I was reminded of this scripture: **"If you harbor bitter envy and selfish ambition in your hearts, do not boast about it or deny the truth. Such 'wisdom' does not come down from heaven but is earthly, unspiritual, of the devil. For where you have envy and selfish ambition, there you find disorder and every evil practice"** (Jam. 3:14-16).

The evil practices were very apparent, and selfish ambition and envy were thriving here. I could still hear the songs of Babylon in the distance and I recalled that the meaning of Babylon is "confusion." The confusion of many people within the lobby was without question, but many were still keeping up a front of success. This also reminded me of a time when Jesus spoke to the religious leaders of His day. He told them that on the outside they looked good, but on the inside they were **"full of greed and self-indulgence."** Jesus told them to **"first clean the inside...then the outside also will be clean"** (Matt. 23:25-26). I knew that there must be a cleansing of our hearts or we too will be guilty of the same hypocrisy.

I asked the Lord, "Is this the disorder your Word speaks of?" That's when I heard a voice speaking to me with a new depth and authority.

Snakes in the Lobby

Disorder will soon be seen by all. There will be much confusion and disorder when the Lord brings His judgment on His people, upon the Great Snakes, and on the Piper himself. Just as if thunder had shook the ground, my whole body vibrated at the entrance of this resounding Voice. It sounded like the voice of my faithful Counselor, but it was different now. It sounded as if it had moved from an internal source to an audible external source. The voice was coming from directly above me. It was so powerful and awesome that I hesitated for a moment in order to brace myself before looking its direction.

Then as I looked, I began to see light, and then more and more light. Soon I felt as if I were looking directly at the sun. And just when I thought I was not going to be able to see anything because of the great intensity of the radiance, I began to see the form of something in the center of it.

Two Large Eyes

All I could focus on was what looked like two very large eyes that were surrounded by a silhouette. My eyes grew accustomed to the light, and I began to see more detail. They were eyes all right—like none I had ever seen. They were wide open. They were huge. As I gazed into them I was

The Vision

stricken with many emotions simultaneously. I was both terrified and exhilarated, and yet apprehensive. The eyes looked like a blazing fire. I began to shake. I was drowning in illumination.

They were the eyes of a great hunter. These eyes were not just full of acute vision; they looked right through me. I became aware of the fact that I was standing in the presence of unending Revelation, Knowledge and Wisdom. My mind could not comprehend or even begin to calculate the depth of this encounter. It felt as if my whole body were ablaze.

I had never felt more exposed or vulnerable before, and I became more afraid of what I was now seeing than anything I had ever seen—even the evil Snakes seemed pale by comparison. I had never felt so small before. I looked away. I wanted to run...to hide...to die. I fell to the ground. It was too much for me—too intense. I was on fire!

Then in a gentle, rolling thunder He spoke, *Do not be afraid. Be at peace now.* It was like water cooling fire.

I felt my senses start to return to me. I began to breathe normally again as the light and the fire turned down to a bearable level. My fear subsided, and I began to be peaceful. After what I had just experienced, I wondered why I had ever been afraid of anything before. I was thankful to still be alive.

"Who...who are you?" I asked, surprisingly calm considering what I had just been through.

The Fear of the Lord

I am THE FEAR OF THE LORD, was the reply. It still sounded like thunder rumbling in the distance. *You have seen but a taste of glory, and you are filled with a holy dread. This is right, for I am to be feared above all. No flesh can stand uncovered in My presence. Now I have prepared you so that you can look upon Me again.*

"No. No. I cannot look," I sputtered with a wave of terror. Although deep inside I was longing to look again, I knew that I was not worthy or even capable of looking upon such splendor. I just wanted to lie there and hide myself. I felt unclean and naked.

I started to worship with my face well covered, when I heard, *Do not be frightened.* The Voice seemed much more gentle this time, almost back to the manner of my Counselor. *You have been pre- pared for My presence by holy fire. You may look to Me now.*

The Vision

As I looked up into the light still hovering above me, I began to see a most amazing sight. "Could it be?" I asked myself. "Could this really be what I am seeing?" I questioned my own judgment. I closed my eyes, took a deep breath and then peered again. Yes it was. It was. What I was looking at was an OWL. It was very large, and astonishingly magnificent. I was filled with wonder.

At first the Owl appeared snowy white, but as the light around it subsided, I could see that it was a shining silver color. It was covered in a beautiful blend of sparkling silver and white feathers. The great eyes that I had seen at first were now very calm and serene. They slowly blinked, breaking up the intensity of their gaze. "How could something so severe also be so kind and...and...pure?" I pondered.

Then as I studied the Solemn Bird further, our eyes locked. My mind was swimming with awe, and I found my mouth beginning to whisper something. "Wi...Wis...WISDOM. Wisdom of the ages!" I proclaimed.

*Yes, **the fear of the Lord is the beginning of WISDOM**, answered the Owl. I am the spirit of Wisdom, he continued. The people have forgotten the fear of the Lord; therefore, they are without wisdom to judge between good and evil. **The fear of the Lord is to hate what is evil**. Without this fear* *there will not be holiness. And without holiness no one will see Him.*

These people flock to His love, kindness and grace, but they have forgotten the Lord's holiness and severity. One must know both the love and the fear of the Lord to truly know Him. They have forgotten that He is a God who punishes sin, and they casually pick and choose only the words they like best. Then the Owl pronounced to the whole room, *Man must live by every word that proceeds from the mouth of God!*

The Wise Owl's silver-white feathers started to stand up at this point. He shifted about and then continued, *Heed the Word of the Lord: Woe to those who do not fear the Lord. They sing of me and use my name and the name of my beloved Son, but their hearts are far from me. They step on one another and exploit each other for their own gain. They lie, cheat and deceitfully flatter one another, and withhold wages that are owed their workers. They live in luxury and have little regard for the weak. They mix the Holy with the profane. All in my name! Away with the noise of their songs! And their false humility!*

If they continue in these ways, I will come on a day when they do not expect me, and at an hour they are not aware of. I will cut them into pieces and assign them a place with the unbelievers! I will separate the wheat from the chaff."

The Great Owl then moved closer and spoke passionately, *The Lord is a God full of mercy and love. But He is also the Righteous Judge who still stands for justice. He will both judge and purify His people with a refiner's fire. He is a consuming fire. All hay, wood and stubble will be consumed. The Lord will have a pure priesthood.* There was a pause. Then he spoke again with a tender voice, *He will have a pure bride.*

I was speechless. These words were like fire, and I am sure I saw tears welling up in the eyes of the Large Owl as he spoke of the pure bride.

The Beginning and the End

"When? When will these things happen?" I asked the Owl.

And this is what he answered: *The tremors have already begun. They can be seen and felt by those who have eyes to see and ears to hear. Seven will be the beginning of the end, and eight will be a new beginning. The Lord will pour out His wrath on those great deceiving Serpents. Soon He will crush their heads. And He will pry the hand of the Piper loose from its control. Their end is near.*

Snakes in the Lobby

I felt as if I were going to fall over at the weight of these great and terrible words. The Wise Owl looked at me and must have noticed that I had begun to reel. *Fear not.* **The God of peace will soon crush Satan under your feet.** *There is nothing to fear—unless you have reason to. There will be terrible destruction for those who are yet under the control of the Serpents when these things happen. Many will suffer greatly at this time. As the wounded Serpents flail in agony, everyone and everything in their path will be in terrible danger.*

"But what will become of us? Is there any hope?" I asked in deep concern.

There was an excited tone in the Owl's response. *The Lord God has prepared His holy army for this time. He will be their refuge and shield, their strength and their song. They are the last-day warriors, equipped with the full armor and the blood of the Lamb. They will be found hidden in Christ and will not love their lives so much as to shrink back from death. For he who wants to save his life will lose it, and he who loses his life for the Lord's sake will find it.*

*Those in this army will be **freedom fighters**. They will carry the power of the cross—the gospel of Jesus Christ—to a dying world. When the Lord gives the command, they will rise up and move out* *from many hidden places as a vast and powerful army. They will be sent to slit the bellies of the Great Snakes and set the captives free in Jesus' name and by the power of His Spirit. And they will be vessels of healing, mercy and love. These His servants will be a standard of Truth and will not compromise His holy Word.*

As the Owl spoke these things, I looked around the lobby and realized that the full-armored warriors were increasing greatly in number just since I had first seen them. They looked strong and ready. A rush of excitement hit me as I saw that the Lord had been preparing His people all along. **"When the enemy comes in like a flood, the Spirit of the Lord shall raise up a standard!"** I shouted, with a rising sense of victory.

The Owl looked almost as if he were smiling at me. *That is right, my son.* The Silver Bird moved closer to me, and I was surprisingly not even nervous at this point. He seemed very approachable now. There was a sweet fragrance in the air. I must have looked quite foolish as I was sniffing repeatedly, trying to take it all in. It was marvelous. Then he spoke again, and the sound of his wise voice shook me out of the almost dream state that I had begun to fall into. Even in the midst of the enemy, the presence of the Spirit of Wisdom was refreshing me.

Snakes in the Lobby

Listen now. You must stay alert. What I speak to you is the truth. You will see this victory over every enemy of the Lord's cross if you continue in Him. He who endures to the end will be saved. All who call upon the name of the Lord will be saved. Many have lost their way, but the Lord has not lost sight of them. He is loving and kind and has compassion on all He has made.

The Lord has let many go their own way, but just as Jonah humbled himself and repented in the belly of the fish, or as the prodigal son repented in the swine pen, so will many of these repent. They are ready to turn from their selfish ways and come home. There will be great joy and celebration in the Father's house. But others will continue in their wicked ways without repentance and they will suffer disaster; still others will escape, but only as one who escapes through fire. These will have nothing to show of eternal value for their lives, because their works have been carnal. Only **"The Spirit gives life; the flesh counts for nothing"** *(Jn. 6:63).*

Mercy Over Judgment

There was a pause. I waited, pondering these things. Then the Silver Bird continued with a quieter tone. *The Lord longs to show mercy to all people, and not judgment. But His judgment is His mercy.*

70

The Vision

*They have not listened to His many attempts to reason with them and have grown callous to His Word. Those who do not love the Truth will be given over to a serious delusion. Soon now the Lord will pour out His wrath so that some might awaken from their stupor, **repent** and be saved. He chastens those He loves, and all He calls His sons.*

Take heed of the word, invitation and blessing of the Lord, *"Those whom I love I rebuke and discipline. So be earnest, and repent. Here I am! I stand at the door and knock. If anyone hears my voice and opens the door, I will come in and eat with him, and he with me. To him who overcomes, I will give the right to sit with me on my throne...He that has an ear, let him hear what the Spirit says"* (Rev. 3:19-22).

"If we deliberately keep on sinning after we have received the knowledge of the truth, no sacrifice for sins is left, but only a fearful expectation of judgment and of raging fire that will consume the enemies of God" (Heb.10:26,27).

Then the Wise Owl leaned over to me and whispered, *You have seen these things as a warning. You are to sound the alarm. Many who now feel comfortable and safe are not. These things were not revealed to you earlier because, as you know, you were still under the control of the Serpents yourself. Because you are learning what it is to fear the Lord, He has revealed these things to you. The Lord confides in those who fear Him. But you must be well warned—if you think you are standing secure, take heed, lest you fall. You have already learned how easily pride and deception can enter your heart.*

I trembled at these words. The Owl spoke. *It is right for you to work out your salvation with fear and trembling, but know that I am with you always, even to the end of the age!*

Then I saw the Glorious Owl begin to spread his enormous wings, each of his feathers gleaming as diamonds. An ominous wind with the power of a whirlwind began to fill the place as these wings began to move. The illumination and majesty was stunning. The great White Owl started to rise into the air. Then the voice that sounded as thunder declared, **THE FEAR OF THE LORD IS THE BEGINNING OF WISDOM...THE FEAR OF THE LORD IS THE BEGINNING OF WISDOM...THE FEAR OF THE LORD IS THE BEGINNING OF WISDOM.** He said it three times, and each time it fell deeper into my spirit, and then settled. I felt changed.

As the Owl slowly rose upward, he spoke these words, *I am the Fear of the Lord. I am the gateway*

The Vision

to wisdom. I have been locked up for many years, but I come now. I am now returning to the church, for the Lord will have a holy people—made in His likeness. As I return to my people, they will begin to see me and know me as I really am. I am the Spirit of Holiness.

I could sense that the Wise Owl was preparing to depart, but I still had much more I wanted to ask him. I blurted out, "What must I do now that I have seen and know these great and terrible things? What should I tell others?"

What has been revealed may be revealed. The time is short. Above all, this is what you are to do: **Love the Lord with all your heart, all your soul, and with all your mind. Worship the Lord your God and serve Him only. This is the one I esteem; he who is humble and contrite in spirit, and who trembles at My Word.** *You must be broken before Him. Everyone who falls on the Rock will be broken, but the one on whom the Rock falls will be crushed. The one who is willing to be broken of his own will and ways, that is the one who is free to fall fully in love with Jesus—the Rock of Salvation. Love your brothers with the same love you have received from the Lord.* **This is my Command: Love each other!**

Come Out!

Then the wind ceased. I looked up and was glad to see that the Wise Owl was still there. Now the Spirit of Wisdom spoke one last time in a loud voice, _**Come out. Come out of her, my people!**_ This time people all through the lobby looked up and heard these words. Everything seemed to stop for a moment. Some people responded immediately to these words, while others acted as if they had not heard and they continued schmoozing even more aggressively. Many others just looked confused.

At this, the Great Owl turned his penetrating glare directly toward the evil Serpents. I saw that Self-Promotion lost its appetite, stopped eating, and began to vomit up its victims; Lust stopped flirting, dancing and biting; Pride and Insecurity finally stopped spinning; the ever side-glancing Fear of Man looked up and froze with holy fear; Jealousy fell to the ground with a great crash; Religion stopped grinning and quickly deflated to the size of one of the small snakes; and black Death turned ghostly pale. They all began to shrink back in terror. Even the smaller poisonous snakes scurried for cover. The more nervous the big snakes became, the more they began to thrash about. The whole place began to shake, and havoc was spilled out all across the lobby. A messy flurry of snake and human activity consumed the place.

I quickly glanced around. Everything had changed. The Piper was nowhere to be seen now. His haunting song had stopped. The now very fragmented parade was dispersing with strife. It was "everyone for himself." What had once looked like unity was now chaos since the Piper's song had stopped. People who were under the control of the snakes were nervously looking about. Even they knew that something was up. I looked back at the Owl. His eyes had become the eyes of a great hunter once again. His wings were held at attention and poised for action, and the huge clawed feet began to open and close and sway with rhythm. There are no words that could describe the intensity of the Owl's penetrating glare—except **"the Fear of the Lord."**

As I watched this scenario unfold, this scripture came alive, **"The Lord will judge His people. It is a dreadful thing to fall into the hands of the Living God"** (Heb. 10:30,31). The Owl looked ready to strike at any moment. Then suddenly the Great Bird was enveloped in a blinding light. There was a powerful sound that stunned my ear drums. It sounded like lasers cutting through matter. I squinted and ducked low to the ground, not knowing what was happening. When the searing sound stopped, there was an unusual but very welcomed silence that infiltrated the place. I looked up and saw something new standing in the Owl's place. The Owl had transformed.

The Dove

It was the most beautiful and graceful creature I had ever seen. It was a DOVE—a pure white dove. Its presence brought serenity and a glorious amber light to the whole place. There was the freshness of a spring day in the air. The exquisite fragrance that I had smelled earlier was now everywhere. It was delightful. All the evil, confusion and deception that once had been so present, now faded far into the distance. It felt as if the power of the universe had filled this very place—and it had. The air was alive with electricity.

My attention was drawn to the fact that the Dove had nine beautiful tail feathers. They were **LOVE, JOY, PEACE, PATIENCE, KINDNESS, GOODNESS, FAITHFULNESS, GENTLENESS** and **SELF-CONTROL.** I could feel all these qualities embracing me at the same time, like a wonderful warm blanket. I was completely at rest and protected. I opened my eyes (not being conscious of when I had closed them) and found I was underneath the wing of the Heavenly Bird. I was sheltered by the power of the Most High. All the hardships and evils of life seemed to have faded far away now. I could have stayed there forever, but the great wing lifted and I stood there under its shadow, gazing with amazement at this Wonderful Bird.

As I looked into its transparent and revealing eyes, there was humility, gentleness and honesty such as I had never seen. Just standing in its presence made me feel more humble than I had ever felt before—as if I had nothing to prove and nothing to lose. This was true freedom. As I continued to gaze into the dark and compassionate eyes, I felt as if I were looking into the eyes of a warm-hearted nurturer. These were the eyes of a Mother. This seemed strange, but it was real. Looking into the eyes of this Holy Bird, I had never felt so fully loved and cared for as I did now.

"Counselor!" I said with astonishment. "You have been with me all of this time!" I couldn't believe what I was now seeing, but I was so thankful. The Dove looked directly at me and nodded slowly. I spilled over with emotion that came on me by surprise. I smiled and teared up at the same time, filled with wonder and awe. This was my Counselor, my Helper, my Teacher, my Friend; but what struck me deepest now was that this was my Comforter. I knew I could not survive for one moment without the help of my Counselor. I was encircled with the revelation of endless love. It was overwhelming. I was safe. Oh how I loved, and was loved by this Graceful Bird.

Then I noticed that its dark eyes looked sad, as if it were carrying some burden on its heart. Our thoughts seemed to become one, and I knew that the burden it was carrying was a burden for mankind. Just being in its presence, I felt it too. Its crystal-like tears fell to the ground. I thought I was going to be crushed with the weight of what I was feeling. It was so heavy. I felt as if I could weep for eternity—for the lost souls of the world. I wanted to run and scream and tell everyone about the things that were now running through my heart and mind; the snakes...the Piper...the armor and the sword...the Lamb that was slain...the cleansing blood...the Owl. But it was too heavy. I couldn't even move. I felt as if my bones were about to collapse under the weight.

A Light Burden

Just then the Dove said, _This is not for you to carry. It is too much for you._ As the Dove spoke, he took one of his feathers and placed it on my shoulders. *But this, my son, is for you to carry. It is light and it is easy. This is what I will accomplish through you, if you are willing. There will be power and grace to accomplish everything that I give you to carry and do.*

The feather fit on my shoulders well. It felt right. It felt good. It wrapped around my armor and hung down like a cape. I was energized, alive and filled with new vision. Then this Scripture came to me with new meaning, **"You will be clothed with power from on high"** (Lk. 24:49).

It felt as if I had been given a piece of the Dove's heart—which I knew was exactly what I had been given, for I felt different. The Dove said, *Look around the room.* I saw everything differently now, but most of all I saw people in a different light. I saw them with heaven's perspective—each and every person had tremendous value and purpose. I was astonished that I had not seen people in this way before. It was so obvious to me now. It was the truth.

Then the Dove spoke these final words, *I tell you the truth, whatever you do for the least of these brothers of mine, you do for Me.* He stretched out his vibrant wings and declared, ***The greatest among you will be your servant. Many who are now first will be last, and many who are last will be first.***

Then the Dove gracefully took off into the air and flew upward toward the high ceiling of the lobby. When it had just about reached the top, the Dove became a ball of blinding light. With the power of lightning and the sound of a great thunderclap, the light fragmented into a myriad of smaller pieces, and fire shot forth into each of the armored warriors that were in the lobby. Then I saw hundreds of white feathers begin to slowly drift downward, resting perfectly on each one's shoulder.

A Heavenly Song

A glorious melody then began to fill the lobby. It was a **Song of Deliverance**. It was the greatest love song I had ever heard. It brought tears to my eyes again, touching me somewhere deep within— moving and refreshing my spirit. I didn't realize how badly I had missed it, or needed it, until I heard it for myself. Warriors all across the lobby were singing. I joined in, surprised that I already knew the words and melody. The music that I was hearing was connecting Spirit to spirit. It was divine. It felt as if the heavens had opened. The fuzzy light was gone, replaced now by the true light. Everything became clear and visible. The great Serpents writhed and twisted in agony at the entrance of this song.

The Vision

The presence and the glory of the Lord swept across the room. It seemed to live within this song. True creativity permeated the room, bringing renewed life and vigor to everyone. I noticed that some of the wounded people I had seen earlier were becoming strong and equipped with full armor as they sang. They began to shine beautifully with the Lord's glory as they continued singing. People weakened and poisoned by snake bites were becoming healthy again as they joined in. There were tears of repentance flowing, and all across the lobby men and women were being set free from bondage.

As people began to regain their sight, they started to flee from the danger of the Serpents. I even saw some of the Snake Keepers breaking free of the shackles that had held them chained to the Snakes. They, in turn, began helping others break free. Once fully liberated, ex-Keepers had great authority to rescue others from the bondage of the Snakes and the Piper, because they themselves were now overcomers.

The intensity and the strength of the song increased. It was tremendous. It was a new song. I could tell that it was resounding, reverberating and resonating across the entire earth. I knew what I was now hearing was the beginning of something that would spread like fire and eventually touch all of mankind. This was God's creativity, and His Spirit literally dwelt in it. All of creation groaned and longed for it. It was true worship. It had the ability to change lives and set captives free—and to create new life. It touched all who heard, but those who sang it from their hearts were truly transformed even as they sang—as they worshiped the Lord.

I could tell that people all around me were falling deeply in love with the Lord, and for the first time I felt genuine love and a sense of community growing in this place. You could feel the Father's love everywhere, and see it shining on people's faces. We were filled with wonder. "This is why we were created," I thought to myself. **"To love and worship God, and to love one another."**

I felt so safe now. The mist of competition seemed to have vanished, and the people began to help and honor one another, even above themselves. My eyes met with the eyes of the brother who had prayed for me earlier. We grinned and nodded at each other. We didn't have to say anything; there were no words to describe what we felt, so we just smiled and sang. Our Father was in control!

Liberty

As the excitement built, a dance of celebration broke out among some of the women who were singing and worshiping the Lord. It was awesome! I felt liberated just watching. I had never seen anything quite like it before, but I knew I was seeing the movements of heaven. It was contagious, and it sent a wave of purity and power across the room. The heaviness that had once hovered over this place lifted, and I was charged with new energy. Before I realized it, I too had joined in the dance, along with many others, and the whole place began to move together as one.

I saw some people begin to run like they had never run before. They did not fear what others thought of them anymore. They were free! All this soon flowed together and evolved into a mighty march that circled and surrounded the place. Strongholds were being demolished! I could feel the walls of hostility and division crumbling down. We were all like children again: laughing, singing, shouting and leaping for joy. Everyone worshiped the Lord in his or her own way. And I heard these great words, **"Where the Spirit of the Lord is, there is liberty"** (2 Cor. 3:17).

Snakes in the Lobby

I was astounded at the magnitude of the transforming power that was being released by this song...this dance...this worship! God inhabited it. It was beyond words to describe. I could hardly believe that I was still in the same place with the same people—but I was. Yet we were certainly not the same! As I stood there in total amazement, I heard my Counselor's familiar voice once again: *I will give you a new heart and put a new spirit in you; I will remove from you your heart of stone and give you a heart of flesh. And I will put my Spirit in you and move you to follow my decrees and be careful to keep my laws (Ezek. 36:26-27).* As I heard these words I understood that this was what was happening to us. There was a softening, strengthening and renewing all taking place in us at once. Only the Spirit could do such a work.

Suddenly I noticed a familiar swirling movement across the floor. There were snakes everywhere. "Oh no! Not here! Not now! Not again!" I was struck with dread. But then I looked again and was amazed to see that as we sang and danced we were actually trampling the Serpents under our feet! This was a war dance—and a Song of Victory. What a feeling it was to worship our great God and King while crushing the enemy at the same time! All the snakes now looked pitiful and helpless. They looked like mere garden snakes in the presence of

The Vision

the Lord, and many of them began to turn on each other. As we unified, the enemy divided. They began to destroy and devour themselves. The entire lobby was set ablaze with the Spirit of Holiness.

I heard a great cry of **"FREEDOM!"** rising up so loudly from the people that it rocked the place! It was awesome. It was like a dream come true. One by one, people continued to join in until it sounded like a thunderous chant. The lobby was engulfed by the song and the cry of freedom as it began to rise to the heavens. I believe I could hear the heavens singing along. The goodness of the Lord could be tasted by everyone; it was like rain falling on well-parched land. I could feel the Living Water of the Spirit pouring out like a great waterfall, refreshing and washing a myriad of dry and thirsty souls. We were flooded with joy unspeakable. The joy of our Salvation—the joy of Life. It brought unity, oneness and peace. But most of all, it brought **Praise, Glory and Honor to the King!**

Then came the GREAT COMMAND. In a loud Voice I heard, *LET MY PEOPLE GO, SO THAT THEY MIGHT WORSHIP ME! So that they might worship Me in SPIRIT and in TRUTH*. And the last thing I saw was the powerful and unified army of holy warriors released to do the Master's bidding. They went rushing forward at the Master's command, with armor gleaming and Swords of

Truth held high. They began to cut people free all across the room.

Then there was silence...and the vision was gone. I heard these final words:

You must overcome and be free of the bondage of sin, self and the world. Be holy as I am holy, for darkness is about to come upon the world, such as has never been seen before. I want My song to be sung, My glory to be known, and My Spirit to be poured out on all people. I am sending My minstrels ahead of My army once again. You must be prepared, purified and made whole to carry this great honor. Many are invited, but few are chosen, because few are willing to pay the price of the chosen. The world will soon be set ablaze with My creativity and My glory. I will inhabit these songs, and the world will taste and see that I am good. I AM the LORD GOD ALMIGHTY, JESUS THE MESSIAH, WHO IS, AND WAS, AND WHO IS TO COME!

A heavenly host began to sing, **"Arise, shine, for your light has come, and the glory of the Lord rises upon you. See, darkness covers the earth and thick darkness is over the peoples, but the Lord rises upon you and His glory appears over you. Nations will come to your light, and kings to the brightness of your dawn"** (Is. 60:1-3).

The Vision

The singing ended with these beautiful covenant words sounding over and over: **"And from everlasting to everlasting the Lord's love is with those who fear Him"** (Ps.103:17).

Part II:
Interpretations and Scriptures

The Lobby. The entrance hall where many people had gathered. They were busy "lobbying" for position, power and their own agendas.

The Snakes. The powerful evil spirits that plague and control much of the Christian music industry and much of Christendom. Each snake represented different sins. They had the authority to control people who had allowed room for these sins to continue in their lives. Whether or not these spirits actually look like snakes, I do not know. But that was the way they appeared to me in this vision. These spirits' primary power is deception. I believe the reason I saw them as snakes is because the serpent was the original "deceiver" from the beginning. Satan is also referred to in the Word as "that ancient *serpent* called the devil, or Satan, who leads the whole world astray" (Rev. 12:9).

The Big One: Self-Promotion. "For whoever exalts himself will be humbled, and whoever humbles himself will be exalted" (Matt. 23:12). The builders of the tower of Babel said this, "Come, let us build ourselves a city, with a tower that reaches to the heavens, so that we may make a name for ourselves" (Gen. 11:4). "No one from the east or the west or from the desert can exalt a man. But it is God who judges: He brings one down, he exalts another (Ps. 75:6,7).

The Charmer: Lust. "Put to death, therefore, whatever belongs to your earthly nature: sexual immorality, impurity, lust, evil desires and greed, which is idolatry" (Col. 3:5). "For everything in the world—the cravings of sinful man, the lust of his eyes and the boasting of what he has and does—comes not from the Father but from the world" (1 Jn. 2:16).

The Two Snakes: Pride and Insecurity. "Pride goes before destruction, a haughty spirit before a fall" (Prov. 16:18). "But blessed is the man who trusts in the LORD, whose confidence is in him" (Jer. 17:7).

The Flesh Snake: The Fear of Man. "Fear of man will prove to be a snare, but whoever trusts in the Lord is kept safe" (Prov. 29:25).

The Green Snake: Jealousy. "Anger is cruel and fury overwhelming, but who can stand before jealousy?" (Prov. 27:4) "A heart at peace gives life to the body, but envy rots the bones" (Prov. 14:30). "Do not let your heart envy sinners, but always be zealous for the fear of the Lord" (Prov. 23:17).

Interpretations and Scriptures

The Small Poisonous Snakes: Bitterness. "For I see that you are full of bitterness and captive to sin" (Acts 8:23). "Get rid of all bitterness, rage and anger, brawling and slander, along with every form of malice" (Eph. 4:31). "See to it that no one misses the grace of God and that no bitter root grows up to cause trouble and defile many" (Heb. 12:15).

The White Snake: The Spirit of Religion. "Woe to you, teachers of the law and Pharisees, you hypocrites! You are like whitewashed tombs, which look beautiful on the outside but on the inside are full of dead men's bones and everything unclean. In the same way, on the outside you appear to people as righteous but on the inside you are full of hypocrisy and wickedness" (Matt. 23:27,28). "You snakes! You brood of vipers! How will you escape being condemned to hell?" (Matt. 23:33)

The Counselor: The Helper, who is the Holy Spirit. "But when he, the Spirit of truth, comes, he will guide you into all truth. He will not speak on his own; he will speak only what he hears, and he will tell you what is yet to come" (Jn. 16:13).

The Armor. The transforming power of the Holy Spirit available to all who are willing to put off the old self and to be clothed with Christ—the full armor of God—so that when the day of evil comes (if it has not already come, it will), they may be able to stand their ground. It speaks of the character of Christ (see Eph. 6:11-18).

The Snake Keepers. The people who have been in power and have, knowingly or unknowingly, let the ways of the world enter into Christian music. "No one can serve two masters. Either he will hate the one and love the other, or he will be devoted to the one and despise the other. You cannot serve both God and Money" (Matt. 6:24). "Turn my heart toward your statutes and not toward selfish gain" (Ps. 119:36).

The Piper. Just as in the fable of old where the Pied Piper led the rats and the children out of the city with a song, so those today that follow the leading of the world or Satan are in nothing but an endless "rat race." This is a picture of the music and media which is misleading our younger generation out of the "city of God," or away from God. I believe that Satan himself has controlled much of today's music. He is believed by many to be the fallen master musician from heaven.

The Owl. This symbol was the most surprising and meaningful to me. The Owl has long been a symbol of wisdom, but as I began to study about owls, I discovered that there is much more to it.

Interpretations and Scriptures

The owl is a friend to the farmer because it feeds on harmful rodents and snakes that would steal and destroy the good seed (the Word) and crop. It can make its approach undetected because its flight is silent. The owl is a bird of prey that mostly hunts at night—in the darkness. Owls have also been called the "night watchmen" because they can literally see in the dark and have incredible, binocular-type vision. Their hearing is also phenomenal—they can detect even a mouse's movement from two football fields away. I believe this acute vision and hearing speaks of the "discernment" which has been greatly missing in the body of Christ. Discernment and wisdom will return as "the fear of the Lord" returns to the church. We have to learn to see even in the dark deception of our day. We live in a time when "even the elect" will be deceived, if that were possible. We desperately need the fear of the Lord and therefore "the spirit of wisdom" to return to us.

The Dove. The Holy Spirit or the Spirit of God.

The Heavenly Song. A picture of the heavenly creativity that God will, and already is, pouring through His purified people to bless both the church and the world. This creativity will bring glory to God and the blessing of His Spirit to mankind.

Scripture References

"Fear God and keep his commandments, for this is the whole duty of man. For God will bring every deed into judgment, including every hidden thing, whether it is good or evil" (Eccl. 12:13,14).

"The eyes of the LORD are everywhere, keeping watch on the wicked and the good" (Prov. 15:3).

"Love the Lord your God with all your heart and with all your soul and with all your mind. This is the first and greatest commandment. And the second is like it: Love your neighbor as yourself" (Matt. 22:37-39).

"The fear of the LORD is a fountain of life, turning a man from the snares of death" (Prov. 14:27).

"And what does the LORD require of you? To act justly and to love mercy and to walk humbly with your God" (Mic. 6:8).

"Today, if you hear his voice, do not harden your hearts" (Heb. 3:7,8).

Part III:
The Renaissance Is Coming

Much to my surprise, the hotel which had been the setting of the *Snakes in the Lobby* vision changed its name. Its name became "The Renaissance." A member of our team looked up the meaning of the word Renaissance, and was amazed to find it defined as "the rebirth, renewal or revival of the arts and literature." The Lord is even writing it on the skyline of Nashville, this city known as Music City U.S.A.: The Renaissance Is Coming!

Change is coming; great change and reform are coming to the church and to the world. Part of that change is the rebirth that is coming to the arts. Creativity will be a powerful vehicle for reaching our culture and the world with the message of Jesus Christ.

Looking back historically to the time known as the Renaissance in the 14th and 15th centuries, this was an era emerging from a thousand-year period of stagnancy called "the Dark Ages."

The Renaissance was a time of great renewal, revival of creativity, enlightened thinking and literature—all motivated by a "pursuit of eloquence."

Snakes in the Lobby

The Greek and Roman classics became a model for eloquence in all areas of life. From these ancient cultures the Renaissance scholars found new inspiration and instruction, and many positive changes occurred which we still benefit from today. This "happy century" greatly transformed government, education and Christian theology, and conceived some of the highest forms of art and music that man has ever known.

While the focus of the Renaissance was on restoring culture, humanity itself became the center of attention. If we took all that the first Renaissance produced and boiled it down into one word, it would be "humanism," which is ultimately self-centeredness. Humanism today has flooded much of our modern culture and has gone on to deny the relevance or even the existence of God.

The Lord began to speak to me saying, *I Am the Creator, the Originator of all things, and I am going to use My creativity to proclaim My holy message to the whole earth.* He said that the Renaissance which is coming this time will not be inspired out of a "pursuit of eloquence" but out of a "pursuit of obedience" to Him. It will not produce self-centeredness, but God-centeredness. The new Renaissance will not bring glory to man, but to God. **"For the earth will be filled with the knowledge of the glory of the LORD"** (Hab. 2:14).

The Wave

As I was praying about this soon-coming Renaissance, I began to see a tremendous vision in the spirit that charged me with great excitement and fear. I saw a massive tidal wave on the rise. As it moved to shore, it built quickly in size and momentum. I knew instantly that this tidal wave spoke of a mighty movement of God. It looked both dangerous and exciting. It was much larger than anything I had ever seen or imagined, and I knew there has never been anything like it before. I was sure that when this wave hit the shore nothing would remain the same—everything would be changed.

I asked the Lord what this was and what it meant, and He said, *This is the moving of my Spirit that is coming upon the whole earth.*

"Men will fear the name of the LORD, and from the rising of the sun, they will revere his glory. For he will come like a pent-up flood that the breath of the LORD drives along" (Isa. 59:19). The breath of the Lord speaks of His Spirit, which moves like a mighty flood.

"And afterward, I will pour out my Spirit on all people. Your sons and daughters will prophesy, your old men will dream dreams,

your young men will see visions. Even on my servants, both men and women, I will pour out my Spirit in those days before the coming of the great and dreadful day of the LORD" (Joel 2:28,29,31).

Obedience Required

I then saw people in the water with surfboards. Some were wading in shallow waters, and others were standing on the beach, but I knew that only those who were in the deep waters would be able to catch this wave. The waters spoke of the Holy Spirit. Then I saw that the surfboards of those who were waiting in the deep waters had the word "obedience" written on them in bright red. Many people did not have boards, and I knew that they would certainly be overcome by what was approaching.

Some were waiting in the waters with all different kinds of surfboards, but they did not have "obedience" written on them. I knew that their hopes of riding this wave would also be futile. It would take great faith to ride this wave, because at first glance many would want to run in fear for cover. One would have to be willing to risk it all (have true faith) to ride this wave. In reality, those who shrunk back in fear were in much greater danger, for the safest place was in riding the powerful crest of the wave.

True Worship, Humility and Brokenness

Just as no surfer would dream of going into the rugged waters of the surf with his hands full, neither can anyone hope to ride this wave with idols in hand. Only true worshipers of God will be able to keep their balance and stay on top of what is coming. We must have no idols before Him! The Lord God must have first place and first love in our lives.

A Webster definition of worship is "extreme devotion and intense love." To worship the Lord means to love Him! Jesus said in John 14:15, **"If you love me, you will obey what I command."** Our obedience is the evidence of true love and devotion (our worship) to God.

I knew when this wave started to break that someone's success in riding it would be all about positioning. If we were in the right position we would catch the ride of our lives, and if we were not, the wave would be devastating. I asked the Lord where we must be when the wave hit. He said that we must be in a position of "humility and brokenness."

I knew then that merely to be in the water (the Spirit), even with our board of obedience, would still not be enough to catch the ride. It would only produce self-righteousness (the worst form of pride) if we were not found in the position of true humility and brokenness, for God only exalts the humble. In order to catch and not be crushed by the power of what is coming, we must be broken of our will and ways, be humble in heart, and committed to radical obedience to the Lord.

"For the earth will be filled with the knowledge of the glory of the LORD, as the waters cover the sea" (Hab. 2:14). This wave will flood the earth with the Lord's glory and the knowledge of Him. It will be a wake-up call first to the church, which is the Lord's mercy. This will not be the final judgment; even though many self-built houses will collapse, this is the Lord's mercy giving people time to repent and rebuild—His way. Jesus said, **"Therefore everyone who hears these words of mine and puts them into practice is like a wise man who built his house on the rock"** (Matt. 7:24). This wave of the Spirit will test the quality of each man's work. Some houses will collapse; some will stand. Whatever is left standing after the impact, God will use to flood the earth with His glory.

God is going to use divine creativity to spread His holy message, the gospel. This will be poured out through His purified vessels, His people. There is a tremendous anointing that is coming, not only on music, but on all forms of art. From Genesis to Revelation we see God moving in creative ways. Creativity is what He ordained and what He enjoys—just as when Solomon was building the temple for the Lord, and it was adorned with the most beautiful visual arts. **"Send me, therefore, a man skilled to work in gold and silver, bronze and iron, and in purple, crimson and blue yarn, and experienced in the art of engraving, to work in Judah and Jerusalem with my skilled craftsmen"** (2 Chr. 2:7).

Divine Creativity Is Coming!

After enduring a stagnant "dark age" of creativity where the best creative work we have done has mostly been cheap imitation of the world, divine creativity is coming back into the Lord's temple, His people. Music and art are primary ways of communicating with our culture. This is the "sound and sight" generation, and art is a language of symbols, sounds and images which can transcend the limitations of the intellect and reach to the heart.

Modern thinking can be rigid with opinions that cause division and factions, suppressing the truth. A verbal or even written message can be rejected or dismissed quickly because of our reasoning or prejudice. But art is not so quickly dismissed. One song or painting can mean a myriad of different things to different people.

Music and art speak as a "language of the spirit" that can penetrate where other forms of communication cannot. A creative expression takes time to be absorbed into any intellectual conclusion, and before the head has time to figure it out the heart can already be moved. I personally have seen the Holy Spirit use music to melt the hardest of hearts—in prisons, clubs, the inner city, and in churches. This allows us to "feel" God's love and presence. We can "taste and see" that God is good. Many times, before the listeners fully understand or even know what to believe, they have experienced a touch from the Lord. The anointed arts are truly one of the most powerful evangelism tools the Lord has given us. Creativity that is born of the Spirit will give birth to spirit. Jesus said in John 3:6, **"Flesh gives birth to flesh, but the Spirit gives birth to spirit."**

The music, dance and creativity of God's people will carry the message of the gospel and the very presence of the Lord to the ends of the earth, for the Lord "inhabits the praises of his people." The Lord loves music. He has chosen it as a way to approach Him. He didn't say to come into His presence with teaching or preaching, but to **"Shout for joy to the LORD, all the earth. Worship the**

The Renaissance Is Coming

LORD with gladness; come before him with joyful songs...Enter his gates with thanksgiving and his courts with praise; give thanks to him and praise his name" (Ps. 100). We are told many times in His Word to "praise his name with dancing and make music to him with tambourine and harp" (Ps. 149:3). In Psalm 32:7 we see that the Lord Himself even sings over His people: "You are my hiding place; you will protect me from trouble and surround me with songs of deliverance."

We are told that the Lord goes into battle and inflicts punishment on the nations to the sound of music: "The voice of the LORD will shatter Assyria; with his scepter he will strike them down. Every stroke the LORD lays on them with his punishing rod will be to the music of tambourines and harps, as he fights them in battle with the blows of his arm" (Isa. 30:31,32).

In Isaiah 42:10,13 we see the Lord Himself will rise to make war and triumph over His enemies at the sound of a praise song that reaches to the ends of earth! "Sing to the LORD a new song, his praise from the ends of the earth...The LORD will march out like a mighty man, like a warrior he will stir up his zeal; with a shout he will raise the battle cry and will triumph over his enemies."

The Counterattack

Satan has constantly used music, media and arts to bombard our the world with an onslaught of his hideously polluted messages. We have seen the moral fabric of our nation be eroded by messages and ideas that often have been first introduced and ushered in by the creative arts. It is now time for a mighty counterattack!

The creative worshipers are the first army that will be sent out for this last battle. Even now, a massive army throughout the world is being purified and prepared to be released into the highways and byways of our cultures. They will be sent forth not in the ways of the world, but in the humility and brokenness of Christ.

The Lord will soon ignite and inhabit all forms of creativity. His people will begin to prophesy through song and dance, to evangelize through film and video, to teach and proclaim the truth through drama and painting, sculptures, multimedia, literature, etc. This will come as a tidal wave like we have never seen before. But this time it will not be celebration of the arts, eloquence or mankind, but of Jesus—our exalted Lord and eternal King. For those who are committed to the **"pursuit of obedience,"** and who above all things will make it their **"goal to please Him"** (2 Cor. 5:9), they are truly in for the ride of their lives!

The Renaissance Is Coming

The rebirth, renewal and revival of the arts is on its way—inspired this time not by ancient culture, but by the God of all the ages and the God of all creativity.

The Renaissance is coming! Let's catch this wave for His glory!

TO ORDER OTHER MORNINGSTAR PRODUCTS:

16000 Lancaster Highway
Charlotte, NC 28277-2061

TO ORDER 1-800-542-0278

PHONE 1-704-542-0278

FAX 1-704-542-0280

SCOTT MACLEOD, a musician and songwriter, is the co-founder of Provision Ministries and The Foundry, an inner-city coffee-house, and is a member of the MorningStar Fellowship of Ministries. Scott's heartbeat is for the true restoration and liberty of the arts and for justice and mercy for the poor. He has also co-founded The Crucible, a training school established so that those who are gifted in the arts can be equipped for ministry.

Scott and his team are currently focusing on restoring an inner-city warehouse called "The Fortress of Hope." This will be a home for the Coalition of Urban Renewal—a team of diverse ministries and churches working together to spiritually and practically rebuild Nashville's inner-city. Scott, his wife Sarah, and their daughter Emily, reside in Nashville, TN.

For more information on Provision Ministries,
The Foundry, or if you would like to be added
to our mailing list for future writings and events,
please contact:

PROVISION/THE FOUNDRY
P.O. Box 22061
Nashville, TN 37202
(615) 327-1200 Provision Offices
(615) 327-4003 The Foundry

THE CRUCIBLE
EQUIPPING FOR CREATIVE MINISTRY

Take some time...to get equipped with biblical foundations and a new perspective on how you and your gifts can be used more effectively for His glory.

WHO?
Creative people who have a heart for ministry—singers, musicians, writers, dancers, visual artists, creative support (business and technical), etc.

WHEN?
Spring and Winter Sessions

COST?
$150.00 per 12 week term

WHERE?
The Foundry, 1419 Clinton Street,
Nashville, TN 37203

No matter where God is calling you ultimately, He wants you to be equipped for the works He has prepared in advance for you (Eph. 2:10). His desire is to grow us up into maturity in Christ, not only so that we may know Him better, but also so we may be more effective witnesses as we use the gifts He has entrusted to us. This is the purpose for The Crucible course.

Space is limited. If you are interested in registering for The Crucible or would like more information, please call: (615) 327-1200.

The Foundry...
As Iron Sharpens Iron

Come worship with us!

The Foundry is a Christian-based coffee house, and is the first ongoing outreach of Provision. It not only provides a creative, spiritual environment in which people are welcome to come and enjoy coffee and music, but it is also a nurturing atmosphere in which people are challenged to go deeper in their relationships with God and others.

Every Friday Night
at 8:00 p.m.
1419 Clinton Street
Nashville, TN 37203
(615) 327-4003

ORDER FORM — PLEASE FILL OUT LEGIBLY

► Questions about your order? Call 1-800-529-1117. ◄

MAIL.

Send order form to:
MorningStar Publications
Order Department
16000 Lancaster Hwy
Charlotte, NC 28277

PHONE.

Order Department:
(credit card orders only)
8:00 a.m. - 5:00 p.m.
Monday - Friday EST
1-800-542-0278

FAX.

Fax order form
24 hours a day to:
(credit card orders only)
1-704-542-0280

METHOD OF PAYMENT:

☐ CHECK / MONEY ORDER

☐ VISA ☐ MasterCard

CATALOG	QTY.	TITLE	COST EA.	TOTAL
		SUB TOTAL		
		NC RESIDENTS ADD 6% SALES TAX		
		SHIPPING AND HANDLING		
		DONATION TO MORNINGSTAR MINISTRIES		
		TOTAL ENCLOSED		

SHIPPING:

Orders	U.S.	FOREIGN
< $10.00	$2.50	$3.00
$10.00 - $24.99	$3.50	$5.50
$25.00 - $49.99	$4.50	$8.00
$50.00 - $74.99	$5.50	$10.00
$75.00 - $99.99	$6.50	$13.00
>$100.00	FREE!	FREE!

FIRST NAME   INITIAL   LAST NAME

STREET ADDRESS

CITY   STATE/PROVINCE   ZIP/POSTAL CODE

DAYTIME PHONE   COUNTRY

☐☐☐☐ - ☐☐☐☐ - ☐☐☐☐ - ☐☐☐☐

SIGNATURE   EXPIR. DATE   /